the making of

A FATHERLESS DAUGHTER

The Book

A Journey of Love, Acceptance and Forgiveness

Compiled By Angela Carr Patterson

Published by:

Oasis Promotions Publishing 4611 Hardscrabble Road, Suite 109-334

Columbia, SC 29229
ISBN-13: 978-1720556398
ISBN-10: 1720556393

Dedication

To the eight authors of this book, we dedicate this project to you. It's because of your courage to share your truth and your commitment to rewriting a new narrative for your lives, that many others will be changed.

To women everywhere who are ready to heal your daddy wounds and begin to live your truth.

To every woman who has ever felt the pain of fatherlessness, we encourage you to take the journey of love, acceptance and forgiveness. It's a journey worth taking.

Special Thanks.

Special Thanks to **Melinda Nazario** for her dedication to editing this manuscript. Your gifts and talents are your amazing contribution to the world .

TABLE OF CONTENTS

INTRODUCTION

I wish I could say that the words Fatherless Daughter didn't exist. Because it does. I wish it wasn't true that millions of girls will go to bed tonight without as much as a good night kiss from their daddy because he's nowhere to be found. But, it is true.

I wish that I could say that I didn't personally experience this incredibly painful hole in my soul from not having my father be there for me. But the truth is, he wasn't there and his absence left an incomprehensible pain and ache in my soul.

We all have a biological father but when the term fatherless is used, it means that the father figure is just not present in the daughter's life. He may be unavailable, unattached or absent. Perhaps he died, may have run away or maybe he's physically present but not attentive and caring. Whatever the reason for a father not being present in his daughter's life, this one key missing element will have many negative consequences as she develops and grows into adolescence and adulthood.

My story began when my mother and father met, got married, then separated during the time my mom became pregnant with me. They later divorced. I never had the pleasure of growing up knowing my father and having a relationship with him. As I became an adult, I went in search to find him, with the hopes that I would finally become a daddy's girl. I did find my father. But, becoming daddy's little girl never became my reality.

I spent years hoping and wishing that my father-daughter-relationship would eventually blossom into a beautiful experience. Only to discover that my father was not capable of such a relationship.

Yet, the truth remained that I so desperately wanted to be daddy's little princess. I longed for his protection, for his provision, his presence and his praise. The thing I missed the most from not having a father around was the feeling of having someone to protect me. Someone who would stand up for me. In many ways today, I still long for that feeling of being protected.

For years, I struggled to make my life work. I struggled to have a healthy sense of self-worth, self-value or self-love. I struggled in my relationships with men and my relationship with money. Because as fatherless daughters, how we do love is how we do money.

My invisible cries in the darkness of my soul went unheard because they were silenced by the pain of rejection and the insurmountable pain of feeling unwanted and unloved by my father.

I remember feeling a sense of loss and not belonging to anyone or anything. I couldn't understand why I felt so alone and as if my life had no real meaning. I later understood that my feelings came from my lack of identity. I didn't know who I was.

We get our identity through our paternal relationships. If that relationship doesn't exist or if it is flawed in anyway, we will experience deep trauma in many areas of our lives.

Emotional and psychological trauma has been defined as the result of extraordinarily stressful events that shatter your sense of security, making you feel helpless and vulnerable in a dangerous world. Lord knows, this is how I felt so many times in my life. Even as a woman, I felt a helpless lack of security and vulnerability with no one to protect me.

This loneliness and fear followed me for years. These feelings dictated the choices I made in my life and many were not in my best interest. It was when my marriage of sixteen years ended, that I began to seek help. I needed to find out why my life had ended up in such a deep, dark desolate space.

My Journey to Being is what I call my healing process. It took years on this Journey for me to begin to heal my daddy wounds, to heal from my broken marriage and awaken to the truth of who I was as a woman. I wish that I could say it was easy. Because it wasn't. But it was simple.

I finally made peace with the truth that my father couldn't give me what I wanted and needed. I also recognized that if I was going to be free from this hole in my soul then I needed to forgive him and allow my broken heart to heal.

As I said before, it took years for me to finally redefine my life beyond my fatherlessness. It took a lot of work for me to understand this journey of love, acceptance and forgiveness. Yet, it was a journey I had to take in order for me to be free.

Today, I spend my time helping women and girls free themselves from the shackles of their daddy wounds, shatter the shame and actualize the power of self-love to create success in their lives.

I do this through my ground breaking work, —The Journey to Being Process designed to help fatherless girls and women heal their daddy wounds through a Journey of love, acceptance and forgiveness.

Little did I know that my fatherlessness would open an entire new world for me and so many women and girls around the globe. The driving force behind my work is that I never want any woman or girl to walk around with a hole in her soul because of her daddy wounds, or from any wound, for that matter.

This book was written to elevate the awareness of the negative impact an absent father can have on his daughter's life once she becomes an adult.

The Making of a Fatherless Daughter book is not about blame. It's about giving women a voice that had been silenced and unheard far too long. It's about telling the truth. It's about shattering the shame and taking a step in the direction to heal and forgive. This book was also birthed to give voice to the silent cries of women who once held a belief that said, —I am invisible and do not exist in my daddy's eyes. As each of these eight women share their stories and their truths, it is our hope that you are moved and inspired to do the same. Each story is different for each woman, but collectively they share a common pain...Fatherlessness.

Truth of the matter is, some fathers don't know how to love their daughters. They abandon them, use them, abuse them, and manipulate them. There's nothing anyone can do to change such fathers. That's just who they are.

But we can change how we feel inside and how we respond to this uncaring behavior of our fathers. We can share our stories to help each other know and understand that we are not alone. And we can change our fate and make it not just bearable, but BETTER all together!

Angela Carr Patterson, Founder of The Fatherless Daughters Network

CHAPTER ONE

THE MAKING OF A FATHERLESS DAUGHTER

Angela Carr Patterson

Pope John XXIII once said: —It is easier for a father to have children than for children to have a real father.

It is not easy to cope with being a fatherless daughter. As females, we crave to be loved, cared for, and cherished by those who brought us into life.

Listen to me: If this is your reality, know that you are not alone. More women and girls are fatherless than you can imagine.

A recent study from Lisa Mancini and Professor Briggs says: —As the divorce rate in the United States climbs to nearly 50 percent, fathers seem to be disappearing from their daughters' lives. Research shows that girls and young women who have an unstable father figure are more liable to have unplanned pregnancy, low self-esteem, high school and college drop-out, poverty, divorce and sexually promiscuous behavior.

A Fatherless Daughter is a female who grew up with an absent, unattached or unavailable father. This one key missing element in a girl's life can have real negative consequences on her as she becomes a woman. The impact of an absent, unattached or unavailable father on his adult daughter's life is critical when it comes to her self- image, her relationship with men, her work, her friendships and even her relationship with money.

When a girl's father makes it clear to her that she is loved unconditionally, for whom she is, and that he approves of her, he begins to lay a foundation for her healthy sense of self-worth, self-love, and self-value, that will follow her into adulthood.

If, however, the little girl does not have such a relationship with the father, if she sees rejection or emotional coldness or withdrawal from him; if he simply is not available and doesn't provide for her needs, her sense of self-worth will be tainted, her self-confidence warped or non-existent. In addition, her portrait of a loving relationship or her image of provisions may become distorted or dysfunctional, and she may find herself - lacking and feeling unsafe and insecure.

There are four primary basic essentials a female needs from her father. She needs his Provision, Protection, Presence and Praise. If these four essential needs are NOT met early on in a girl's life, once she becomes an adult, she begins to feel unsafe, insecure, unwanted, unloved and rejected. There begins the —Making of a Fatherless Daughter Woman.

CHAPTER TWO

BEYOND FATHERLESS

Melinda Nazario

"He didn't want you... He asked me to have an abortion." That was the answer my mother gave me when I asked why I didn't have a father. I was seven. I met him for the first time when I was three. It was such a quick occurrence, it was almost as if it never really happened. We were living with my grandparents in an apartment that sat on a corner above a liquor store. The doorbell rang, and Mom went down the elongated staircase to see who was at the door. I was sitting across from Grandpa at the dining room table. He was reading the sports section of the Chicago Tribune, and I was skimming through the comics. Mom called me from the bottom of the staircase with such an urgency in her voice. I ran to meet her, and my pace was interrupted when I saw her forehead wrinkled in confusion and arms crossed over her chest, as she stared intensely to her left. I placed my hands on both sides of the doorframe and looked to my right. I saw the profile of a man leaning against the building with one leg propped up. He turned to me and smiled. He had a dark brown goatee, long, dark curly hair that was slicked back with an immense amount of gel, a tiny gold cross earring dangling from his left ear, faded jeans, and white gym shoes.

"This—this is your *father*, Mama," my mother said awkwardly.

I couldn't even register what that word even meant. I remember him looking at me with this anxious expression, like he wanted and needed to do something for me in that very moment. He took off his earring to give it to me, and Mom told him that I didn't have my ears pierced.

"She looks like me," he said as he kept smiling.

I heard those words before from several family members. I couldn't agree or disagree with them, but even with him standing there in front of me with those familiar eyes and lips identical to mine, I didn't see it. I didn't wanna see it. I looked like my mom and no one else.

The visit was short. I thought about it for a few days, but his presence faded once again, and years passed without him trying to reach out to the girl who looked like him.

He reappeared when I was eight. By that time, Mom got married to my stepfather, had two boys, and got divorced. We were living in a low-income apartment, and he came to visit a handful of times. I showed him my room and my wall filled with awards, but it wasn't enough to keep him. He disappeared again. My stepfather also vanished, but I was glad he did. He used to beat my mother, and at that age, I started to see there was no point in having a man in the house. They never stay, and when they do, they hurt you.

Growing up, I didn't wanna face or admit how my father's absence affected me. It was also a complicated situation because I stepped into the role of a second parent within the household to help my mom and to keep the family together. When my stepfather left, my mother was broken. Helping her and keeping my family together was the only thing on my mind, so I locked away my true feelings. Over the years, I began to develop such a hatred towards my

father. Every Father's Day that passed was a reminder of what I didn't have, and I began overcompensating. I took care of my family. I turned into the "man of the house," and my siblings knew I was the one enforcing the rules in the home. It made me feel good for many years, because I felt it was my way of showing my father and every other man that I didn't need them. I could survive without them, and I could do their job better than they could.

When I entered my teen years, things became more complicated. I didn't trust men, but I couldn't fight the fact that I was attracted to boys and wanted their attention. The first time I felt wanted by a boy was when I was 15. He was 18, cute, and dangerous. His attention and affection made me overlook all his bad qualities. He was a drug dealer, a cheater, and extremely possessive. I lost my virginity to him because I thought that his controlling behavior was love. I thought that he loved me so much, he didn't want to share me with anyone else. Little by little, I had no friends and he even controlled when I could come outside. It was insane. I was so foolish, but I didn't know any better. At least he was there. At least he wanted me.

That relationship lasted for a year, until the day I surprised him at his house and another girl answered the door. She looked at me, up and down, and asked why I was there. I saw the girl a few times before. She was the younger sister of one of his friends. At that moment I realized how he enjoyed going after young girls because of how innocent and naïve they were. I told her I was there for Jorge. She said that he told her we broke up. She let me in and we began comparing stories. We were each sitting on sofas that sat across from each other, and when he came in, he paused, sat next to her, and greeted her with a hug and a kiss.

"What's up, baby?" He said to her, nonchalantly.

"She's saying that you're still with her."

"She's lying, baby," he said, with a straight face.

I got up from my seat and began picking up my belongings that were there: My CD player, CDs, and t-shirts. I walked out and couldn't help but think about how I could've been better. Was this all my fault? Was there something I could've done for him? Is there something about me that just isn't enough?

A year later, I got into another relationship. It honestly wasn't any better. He was a gang-banger, and he ended up in jail 6 months into our relationship. He was sentenced to 10 years, and I stayed with him for three of those years. At that time, I didn't know why I decided to stay, but as I got older I realized why. While he was locked-up I knew he couldn't technically cheat on me with another girl. The jail mail was also so intense. I would receive 10+ pages every week filled with words that expressed how special I was to him, how much he loved me, and wanted me to be his wife. I loved being loved by him, and I didn't want to let it go. I also enjoyed the fact that I was only able to see him once a week, and then once a month when he got sentenced to a state penitentiary. It was like the best of both worlds for me. I was receiving all this "love," but I still had my space, which was great for me because I didn't really know how to have a man be a part of my everyday life. Two years into the relationship, he showed me a tattoo on his wrist with my name on it, and he thought it would be a great idea for us to get married. I was 18, and I agreed. The following week I got his name tattooed on my lower back and surprised him with it. We agreed to write to a judge to ask permission to get married while he was still incarcerated. I was 18 and ready to sign up for a challenging future simply because the idea of him wanting to be with me forever made me feel so special.

My father's absence affected me more than I wanted to admit. I wanted a man's love, and I wanted to prove that I could be enough to make someone stay. I didn't know what a real man looked like. I didn't know that men could be any better than what I was exposed to.

Although I was still angry with my father, I began to wonder what life would be like if he was around. I started to feel confused about my life and knew I needed some direction. I locked myself in my room and began to pray to God for the first time in a long time. I told God that I wanted to see my father, and I wanted to see if there was any chance I could have him in my life. I wanted to know the other side of my family tree. Not only did I not know him, I didn't know my grandparents, aunts, uncles, or cousins. For all I knew, I could've ended up falling in love with my cousin and not even have known it! But in all seriousness, my prayer was so intense that night. I just wanted to see if I could have a second chance at being a daddy's girl. A month later, I was running some errands for my mom and ended up in our old neighborhood—the one we lived in when I was three. It was a very hot summer day, and I went into a familiar grocery store to get something to drink. The owner of the store, Patrick, recognized me. I remember seeing him a few years before that. He knew everyone from my mother's side of the family. He asked me how my mother was doing and also asked about my grandparents. I updated him on everyone. Just as I was about to end the conversation, he told me that he recently saw my dad. I must've made a crazy facial expression, because his face immediately changed from a smile to a look of confusion.

"Did I say something wrong?" He asked.

"No, I—I just haven't seen my father since I was eight." I responded as I looked down at my shoes.

"Oh, I'm sorry. I didn't know."

"It's ok, how could you know that?"

"Umm, I have his number... Do you want it?"

My heart immediately started racing. I froze for a moment and didn't know what to say.

"It's actually in the store's system. He's a preferred member. I'm really not supposed to do this, but I'll give it to you if you want it," he continued.

"Sure. I want it."

I stood there in awe. *Maybe there is a God,* I thought to myself as he went to copy down the number. He handed me a folded yellow sticky note. I grabbed it, thanked him, and left. I held onto that number for two months, completely terrified to see what his reaction would be. I finally mustered up the courage and dialed the number, but it went to voicemail. I didn't leave a message and I couldn't bring myself to try again. A few days passed, and his number lit up the screen on our cordless house phone. My mom answered, and it was my grandmother on the other end. The number belonged to my grandparents; he lived in their basement. She told my mom that she recognized the last name on the caller ID and couldn't believe her eyes. She said she always thought of me; I was their only grandchild. My father wasn't home at the time, but she said she would tell him I called. Later that evening the phone rang. My heart felt like it was about to beat straight through my chest, and I had an intense knot in my stomach. I answered and heard his voice respond to my hello. There was awkward silence between our greetings and we both hesitated every time we were about to say something. It was weird, to say the least.

"I'm actually glad you called, but how did you get my number?" he asked. "I've been thinking about you and didn't know where to begin to try and find you," he continued.

I told him how I got his number, and he laughed. He thought it was pretty crazy too. There were more awkward pauses and then I finally got straight to the point.

"Why did you leave me?"

"To be honest... I thought you would be better off without me. I don't know how much you know about me, but I was heavy into alcohol and some serious drugs. I knew I wasn't gonna be any good for you, so I stayed away."

I remained silent.

"But I've been clean for some time now, and that's why I've been thinking about looking for you."

"Mmm."

He hesitated, but went on to ask, "Do you have any plans for tonight? I would love to pick you up and take you out for pizza, so, you know, we can talk face-to-face."

"That would be cool," I responded, trying not to sound too eager.

Within an hour he was at my front door.

"Wow, you're a woman!" He said as he stared at me in amazement.

"Well… That's what happens when 18 years go by," I responded, sarcastically.

We went to Mama Luna's Pizzeria, and my mom and my brother, Giovanni, came along.

By the end of the night he told me that he had a girlfriend named Michelle and she was a few months pregnant. He told me that he really wanted to be a part of my life and he wanted me to be a part of his.

Things started out great. He would call me several times a week and I would spend the weekends at his house to be with him and my grandparents. He eventually moved into his own apartment—with Michelle and her eight-year-old daughter, Andy—a few months before the baby was born. I helped them on moving day and couldn't help but notice how he went out of his way to set up Andy's room. He bought her a brand-new bedroom set, a desk, a computer, and a TV. I'm not gonna lie, I was jealous. I never got that treatment from my father, and this girl, who wasn't even his, was getting the better version of him. I never voiced my opinion, though. I just kept telling myself to be grateful.

A few months later, my new baby sister, Angelina, was born. I was getting used to spending the weekends with them. We would go out for breakfast and go to different places around the city like the Air and Water show, Navy Pier, and the zoo.

My life was changing. I was changing. And I wasn't sure about spending the rest of my life with Tony anymore, so even though I still loved him, I made the decision to end the relationship.

Just when I was getting comfortable with having my father in my life, things began to change. As we entered our second year, the calls gradually declined. When I would call him to ask about coming over, he always had an excuse for why I couldn't. I brushed it off and put all my focus on embracing my new single life with plenty of parties and liquor. At the time I was working as a Certified Nurse Assistant and I would hang out with my coworkers after work; they were all older than me. They managed to get me a fake ID, so I could go bar hopping with them, and that's when I fell in love with the attention I received from dressing all sexy and getting drinks from all the guys. That phase led me to my next boyfriend, Nefty, who would later end up being the father of my child. After being in a "relationship" with a jailbird for three years, it felt good to have someone physically there. I started to feel like I could do the real relationship thing. Our relationship progressed quickly; too quickly. I met him in May of 2005 and by October 2005 I was pregnant. When I told him the news, he freaked out, but he told me he would be there.

I went on to tell my family, and I told my father. About a month later he picked me up on a Saturday by himself. I found it strange that Michelle, Andy, and Angelina were not in the car. He was weird. Quiet. I couldn't take the awkward silence anymore, so I finally asked,

"What's wrong? Where are we going?"

"Melinda, we have to talk."

He parked the car, turned off the ignition, and just sat there looking down at his lap.

"What is it?" I asked.

"I don't think we can hangout anymore."

"What?! Why?!"

"Michelle says we're spending too much time together."

"Are you serious? I didn't have you for 18 years!"

"I know, Melinda. I really messed up with you, but I don't want to mess up with Angelina."

"I'm not understanding any of this."

"Michelle keeps giving me a hard time. She feels like you're coming between our family. She's threatening to leave. I didn't get to be there with you every day, and I'm sorry about that. But I don't wanna miss out on being there with Angelina."

"So, that's it? I just get thrown aside. AGAIN!"

I got out of the car with tears running down my cheeks and a weight of disappointment on my shoulders.

I kept trying to call him and left him countless messages to try to get him back in my life. I know it was naïve of me, but I thought that with me having a baby, he could make up for lost time through building a relationship with his grandchild. I was four months pregnant when he finally called me back.

"Hey!" I answered.

"What do you want?"

"Umm, I just wanted to see if you have some time to hangout this weekend."

"No, Melinda. I already explained the situation to you."

"Yeah, but I"—

"But nothing, Melinda. Damn! You're a grown woman, you don't need a father!"

There was a dead, cold silence that was broken abruptly by my cry. I didn't need a father growing up, and I didn't need one now, so when was it gonna be the right time for me to have one?

That moment hurt more than him not being there at all during my childhood. When I was younger, I used to always think to myself that if he got to know me, he would love me, and he would be there for me. But to have him walk out after getting to know me, to see how easy it was for him to throw me away, broke me and made me feel worthless.

Nefty and I moved in together and tried to be a complete family for our baby girl, Kailah. He was a great father, but he was not that great at being my partner. We were young, and we both had our issues, and we both took those issues out on each other. I tried to make it work so that Kailah could have a "real" family, but we brought out the worst in each other. So, we ended the relationship, but he continued to be an active father and remained involved in our baby girl's life. I'm beyond grateful for that.

For years I didn't talk about my father. I just tried to erase the memories and act like I wasn't affected by his absence at all. But it really did affect me. After Nefty, I didn't want to get into another relationship. I had my moments where I wanted to be with someone, but I would either pick a guy that wasn't ready to commit, or I would be the one playing games.

In 2011, my grandpa from my mother's side became very ill. He had Lymphoma cancer and knew his final days were approaching. One night, he asked everyone to come to his home. I was sitting on the side of his bed with my cousins, Sarai and Jacky. My grandma was standing by the door frame, and he motioned her to come closer. He grabbed her hand and told her how much he loved her. As I listened to them reminisce about the life they built together, I felt my emotions rip through my numb state of mind. For the first time in a long time, I cried. I opened myself up in that moment and realized how much I really wanted that. I wanted something real. I wanted to build with someone. I wanted to really know what it felt like to love someone and to have them love me back. But I couldn't have any of that without making peace with my fatherless situation. I was too afraid of being hurt, of being left, of being abused, and I needed to overcome it all.

A month later, my cousin from my father's side, Maria, called to let me know that my grandfather passed away. I was still mourning the death of my other grandpa, and didn't really know how to process the news. She told me that my grandmother wanted me to attend the funeral services. A part of me didn't want to attend because five years had already gone by since the last time I saw anyone from that side of the family, including my father. But I decided to go and pay my respects. I walked into the funeral home and of course, the first person I saw was my father. He was sitting on a brown vintage couch with Michelle and they both looked surprised. They then immediately looked away. I took a deep breath and walked into the viewing room. I went straight to the front and sat next to my grandmother. Within minutes I heard loud voices coming from the hallway. My grandmother went to see what was going on. My aunt sat next to me and told me that my uncle and father were arguing because of me. My father told the rest of the family that if I didn't leave, he was going to leave. My grandmother yelled at him and told him that I had every right to be there. He didn't agree, and so he left his own father's funeral. I was stunned. I couldn't believe that he didn't want to see my face that bad that he left the funeral home before the service for his father even began.

I felt every eye in the room on me, and I immediately wanted to just run out of there, but my grandmother grabbed my hand and told my aunt to start the slideshow. It was about five minutes long, and it was filled with pictures of my grandfather and the entire family. Holidays, birthdays, and random BBQs; I wasn't in any of them. I felt so out of place. These people are my blood, yet there is no connection.

That was the last time I saw anyone from that side of the family. I learned to let go of people who refuse to make an effort to be in my life. I also learned that day that I will always be a fatherless daughter.

In 2014 I met the man that I'm still with today, Joe. I knew instantly that things would be different with him. I felt how much he valued me with every kiss, conversation, and gesture. I didn't realize how deep my fatherless wound was until my relationship with Joe began to grow. As we became closer, my issues came straight up to the surface. I was terrified of him leaving me. When he would go out to an event, I would freak out and think that he was gonna meet another girl that would have the power to make him leave me, the way my father did. My defining moment was realizing that I was feeling that way because I didn't know my worth. I was still holding on to the fact that I was worthless, and that anyone out there was better than me and it was just a matter of time for the guy I was with to see that. I also realized I tied my value to the things I could offer. I had a nice car, a great paying job, a nice apartment, and I would dress nice.

A year and a half into our relationship, I made a career change. Joe was truly supportive and agreed that I needed to do what made me happy. So, I pursued a career in writing and I took a huge pay cut, and it really began to mess with the way I viewed myself. I didn't feel like I was on top of my game and I felt worthless. Normally I would keep my feelings to myself, because I didn't want anyone to know my insecurities, but I felt like I could tell Joe anything, and so I did. He hugged me so tight that night and said,

"I love you, baby. I love you because of who you are, not because of what you do or have."

Those words replayed in my mind over and over again. *I love you for who you are.* I thought to myself, who am I? I had confused my identity with titles, accomplishments, and awards; I dismissed the fact that I was valuable before any of those things were added to my name. I realized that I had been reverting back to that little girl in my room who was trying to show her father all her awards to see if they'd make her seem good enough for him. And because of that, every time I didn't have anything to offer or any time I wasn't accomplishing anything new, I felt worthless.

I had to let it all go. My father will never love me. He will never want me. He will never accept me. But I have finally found the strength to love, want, and accept myself. Beyond my fatherlessness, I am so much more. Beyond my accomplishments, my titles, and my awards, I am one hell of a woman. I am beautiful, thoughtful, inspirational, strong, brave, funny, caring, smart, and I am fulfilling my purpose in this world.

The Impact of Melinda's Story on Your Life

What moment in this story resonated with you the most?

____

____

____

____

____

____

How has this story impacted you?

____

____

____

____

____

____

Melinda Nazario

Melinda Nazario is a writer, singer, and source of inspiration, born and raised in Chicago, IL. Between the ages of three and eight, she began to express her love for music, reading, and writing, and eventually ventured off into writing stories and songs of her own. She was determined to make a living using her creative gifts. However, unforeseen circumstances brought her goals to an extended pause. Her mother became ill, and there wasn't a second parent present in the household. As the eldest, out of four, she took on the responsibility to care for her mother and siblings. It took quite a few years for her family to regain stability on their own, but when they did, Melinda decided to begin a new chapter in Orlando, FL. After taking some time to reflect and after an extensive hiatus, she now has returned to her passions as awiser, stronger, and focused woman, ready to make her dreams a reality. Using her writing skills and vocal talent, she is determined to inspire people with her story. Melinda speaks on her challenges with being a fatherless child, choosing the wrong men, motherhood, cutting out toxic friendships, and breaking free from her limited existence.

Chapter Three

I Am a Fatherless Daughter

Lakeisha Hankins

"I had buried the pain so deep, I didn't even know it existed."

I am a fatherless daughter; I can finally utter the words out loud. I never spoke those words because I was afraid of hurting my mom and my stepdad (who I call dad). My parents loved me unconditionally, so I learned to be content with not having a relationship with my biological father.

My mother had me at the age of sixteen. My first memory of my biological dad was when I was around the age of eight. For several years, he wasn't sure if I was his child or not. So, with this in mind, I never put all the blame on him for not being around because I felt my mother played a role in his absence. As the years passed, he became aware that I was in fact his child so, it was then up to him to make an effort to be a part of my life. But he never did. And I was left wondering why he wouldn't fight for me.

As a child, I was quiet and unable to communicate my feelings. To be honest in my house we didn't talk about feelings, we weren't allowed to have feelings. Quite frankly, no one gave a damn about feelings. With this type of environment, it never seemed like an appropriate conversation to bring up, but as I progressed in my teen years, I began to struggle more so with not having the presence of my father in life. He periodically made appearances throughout my life, I mainly saw him because of the communication he continued with my mom, but me, alone, just wasn't enough for him.

As I grew into my late teens, my self-esteem diminished. Even with the love I received from my mother and stepfather, I lacked self-worth. I began to seek attention and validation from boys who were much older than me and began noticing me, and I found myself on a path of destruction where I was in search of love in all the wrong places. I became very promiscuous and rebellious towards my mother and my actions resulted in a teenage pregnancy.

At the age of 16, I became a single mother and I had to fast track myself to adulthood. I knew for sure that I didn't want a relationship with the father of my child. Because of that decision, he refused to have anything to do with me, including our daughter. I was suddenly a fatherless daughter raising a fatherless daughter.

My circumstances taught me to be independent and strong. I learned that men weren't responsible or trustworthy. To top it off, I would hear words from my stepfather like, "Don't ever depend on a man; the only person you can depend on is yourself." I adjusted and carried on. Masking the pain had become my new normal.

I carried this silent pain for so long, and solely focused on providing for my child, finishing high school, and going to college to get my accounting degree. When I graduated from college, at the age of 21, I met my now-husband. He was a single father and our daughters were the same age. I admired how he made an effort to provide for his daughter and remain in her life. This quality made him so attractive to me. We began dating and two years later he proposed. Things moved very quickly, and my emotions were torn between being in love and having a family.

One week before the wedding, he called it off because of trust issues. A few days later, I found out I was pregnant with his child so, we made an effort to make the relationship work. Two years later we had another child and seven years into the relationship we got married. I was content with marrying him; it seemed like the next step since we had made a family.

I thought I was in a good place mentally and emotionally until I relocated to Georgia to further my career. Financially, it wasn't an easy move as my husband was unemployed,. so I focused on starting a business to earn extra income. In the process of building a business, joining a ministry to empower women, and finding a home church, I embarked on this journey of discovering my purpose. I realized that I didn't know who I was and that I was unhappy and as a result, my life was a hot mess.

Everything looked good on the outside. I was staying in a relationship that was unfulfilling for all the wrong reasons. I was scared that if we were not together, he would not be there for his girls financially and emotionally. I was also playing it small in my business by chasing money instead of purpose. I knew what I was called to do but I was running from it, because how could I tell other women to go after their dreams when I wasn't ready to do the same? I kept dancing the same old dance, trying to make it work, trying to uphold this image, because I didn't want to look or feel like I failed.

I tried to avoid the pain by putting all my energy into building my business and establishing my identity in that way. Eventually, making a consistent income became a struggle, and I stopped showing up. I felt stuck. I realized not only was I not showing up in my business, I wasn't showing up in my life.

I shut everything down. I left the ministry, I shut the doors of my business, and I stopped being busy with the kids' activities. In the midst of my quietness was where God began to work on my heart and remind me of who I was in Jesus Christ. I was reminded that I had value, I was worthy of love, I was fearfully and wonderfully made, and my pain was all for a purpose. In that moment of transformation, I realized how God uses people to speak life into you and to confirm what he has already said. HE used Angela Carr Patterson and for years she has planted seeds in my life, spoken words to me that made my soul cry, and challenged me to stand in my truth. Little did I realize the Lord was repositioning me.

My independent personality, courage, strength, ambition, never-ending journey to success, and self- growth became my greatest allies. My fear of abandonment, and my ability to mask the pain became my enemy because I confused being content with settling. I took time to reflect back on my life. My past was the key to my future and what I saw was a recurring pattern. I was hiding my pain behind my ministry, marriage, kids, work, and business. I didn't know who I was because I was too busy being who I thought I needed to be.

I spent time journaling and reconnecting with my true authentic self. My life experiences, choices, and behaviors had affected me in more ways than I could have ever imagined because I was too busy being strong to notice. I realized I needed to make peace with my past and forgive my father for his absence and accept the fact that I may never receive his apology. I had to also forgive myself so that I could walk boldly and purposely in my future.

I don't have a relationship with my father but my heart is open to having one with him. I made a bold decision to love myself and I realize now that I don't have to be anybody but me. I have learned to know that God's love is healing. He never leaves us, or forsakes us, and we can always put our trust in him. God used my pain to ignite a passion and fire within in me to be able to share my story to other fatherless daughters, and to remind them that they are enough, they are never alone, and they can move forward in their power.

The Impact of Lakeisha's Story on Your Life

What moment in this story resonated with you the most?

____

____

____

____

____

____

How has this story impacted you?

____

____

____

____

____

____

Lakeisha Hankins

LaKeisha Hankins is a Woman of God, a devoted wife, and mother of 4 beautiful girls. She is a Passion Strategist, Certified Life Reposition Coach & Fatherless Daughter Advocate. She specializes in empowering women entrepreneurs to Unleash their Truth and Unlock their Success. She offers a solution-focused approached to turning your passions into profit and teaches simple, practical proven strategies and life principles to help her clients get the results they want in their business and life.

CHAPTER FOUR

FINDING PEACE WHILE SEARCHING FOR LOVE

Tonya Hart

My entrance into this world was a clear indication of the kind of life I was about to endure. Born at 7 months, weighing only two pounds, and not expected to survive, I was welcomed by my 17-year-old mother. I was a secret up until she reached her sixth month. She was terrified to tell her parents, and as a result, never received proper prenatal care.

During the early part of my life, images of my father were quite vague. I don't remember our first meeting, but I do remember the one time he called me on my birthday. When I was three, I moved to Savannah to live with my paternal grandmother. I thought that by living with his mother, I would then have a relationship with him. However, that did not happen. He would come home, and it was like we were strangers. He never attempted a conversation with me or showed any type of emotional connection towards me. Even when he called, I knew that my grandmother was talking to him, but he neither asked to speak to me nor did she encourage him to talk to me. After a while, I began to develop such a resentment towards him, causing me to ignore him each time he was home.

From what I know, he spent most of his life in and out of jail and prison for drugs and domestic violence. Straight out of high school, he married his girlfriend at that time who was pregnant with his second child. They followed his older sister to Detroit, then they ended up in Texas, where they had their second child together. My first recollection of seeing him besides him visiting the home in Savannah, was when I was 10 and went with my grandmother to visit him in Texas. He had separated from his wife and was living with his new girlfriend, Gloria, who was pregnant with my sister. During our visit, Gloria was very nice to me and I remember thinking about how pretty and kind she was. They were polar opposites, and we later found out that he was being physically abusive to Gloria. Because of all the drama they had going on, they sent my little sister, Erica, to move to Savannah with me and my grandmother. Even though Erica was 10 years younger than me, I felt smaller and insignificant compared to her. There was something about her that made Jimmie (my dad) want to call and check up on her. Yet, after their little conversation would end, it never crossed his mind to ask her to pass the phone to me.

I grew envious of her. She absolutely loved Jimmie and would tell him everything that I did to her that she didn't like. He would then create time to get on the phone just to scold me and tell me to let her do what she wanted. I would intentionally not do what he said because he loved her and not me.

It was Christmas time and Jimmie and Gloria came home to visit like they did every year. During the visit, he got into an argument with Gloria and it quickly escalated. He beat her in such a way that an emergency visit to the hospital was needed. I saw his true colors and I began to hate him even more. My grandmother tried to talk to him repeatedly about his behavior, but he never changed.

As a teenage girl, I began to have feelings of insecurity and low self-esteem. I felt like I wasn't pretty, was too skinny, not smart, and just out of place, as most of my friends were from two-parent homes, and I lived with my grandmother. When I was in the 7th grade, I met a boy who was a few years older than me. He showed interest, and I believed we were in a relationship. We did all the things people do in relationships, including sex. I clung to him thinking that he truly cared for me. I couldn't see it then, but whatever it was that we had was far from a relationship. It was just a sexual thing, and he was doing it with other girls in the neighborhood too. He never took me out on dates, and he never displayed any type of affection towards me. But I settled for what I could get from him and played this role with him on and off until I graduated from college. This was just the beginning of my aimless pursuit for love.

In between my time with him, I met another older boy. He was in the 12th grade while I was in 9th. At first, it seemed like a good relationship. It was a step up from the previous one. We weren't able to go out on dates all the time, but he would visit me and spend a lot of time with me at school. It then turned sexual, quickly. One day he asked me to have sex with his friend to prove that I loved him! I didn't even consider that, and quickly broke up with him. Years later, when we were adults, he called me to apologize for the way he treated me and said that I was a nice person and didn't deserve it.

During the summer of 11th grade, I fell in love. He came from a good family where both of his parents were college educated and successful. He was the nerdy type but also played football, was a genuinely nice and thoughtful young man. I was his first girlfriend. We spent the summer together and it was wonderful. When 12th grade started, he suddenly became attracted to another classmate. My insecurities began to manifest and all I could think about was how she was much prettier and smarter than I could ever be. I don't know why, but I told him he could sponsor her for homecoming and she then began to turn her attention towards him romantically. I felt that they had more in common and that she was a better choice for him than me. I felt that he was too good for me and that I didn't deserve someone like him so, I broke up with him. I then found out that they started dating, and I was completely devastated.

While in college, I dated, but not seriously like the other girls. I wore my heart on my sleeve and thought that if a guy paid me any type of attention, that it was genuine. During these college years, I somehow became pretty, smart, and witty. I continued to date guys that were 3+ years older than me. For some reason I thought older men would treat me better. I also developed an attitude that I would not let a man control me or treat me the way Jimmie treated women. My exterior was now considered pretty, soft, and fragile, but my interior was cold and mean-spirited. I was in complete control. I broke up with men on the spot if they said or did anything that I didn't like. They would call to apologize, but it didn't matter to me. I would move on to the next guy because I always had someone wanting to date me. The guys would also call my grandmother and talk to her about what happened and try to convince her to talk me into getting back together with them. I didn't have a problem getting a boyfriend, but keeping one was a challenge. Most times, I didn't care. I felt that college for me was a means to success, not marriage, unlike other girls who planned to get engaged while in college or soon after.

I attended graduate school but didn't date at all, as I was really focused on my studies, graduating, and then getting an excellent job. After graduate school, I met and fell for who I thought was the love of my life. I was so infatuated with him that I finally let myself go. I have never been the jealous type and I was sort of naïve as I never thought that any man would cheat on me. He was a police officer and the most handsome man in the world to me. I had gained confidence in myself because of my degrees but still not totally in my self-worth. I was so happy with him. This was my first real adult relationship. We traveled, I spent every weekend at his house, and we did all types of activities such as professional sports games, hanging out with friends and family, and spent most of our free time together. I was on cloud 9 for 10 months. This was even though everyone told me that he was cheating on me with multiple women. He always had a good reason to explain away the "rumors" and I always forgave him.

I was offered a job in Miami, FL in 1994 and accepted. I asked him to move with me and he declined. He then said that since I was moving, we needed to break up. This was before I was even given a start date. I was devastated and heartbroken. It was January when I was offered the job, but I didn't start until June that year due to a hiring freeze. I thought that we would still be together during that time, but evidently, he had moved on. I caught him with a woman at his security job and found out that his car which his sister was supposed to be using, was being used by another woman. There were other instances of him and other women and by the time I moved to Miami in June, we weren't even on speaking terms.

I moved to Miami with the hope that it would be my new awakening and that I would finally release all the insecurities I felt about myself. But instead of focusing on me, I began to date again, loosely. It didn't take long for me to repeat my patterns, and I was once again in a sexual relationship, hoping that it would eventually become more. He was an older doctor that I worked with at the hospital and made it very clear that we would not have a real relationship. This pattern continued of just dating with no real intention to grow. I never felt that any of the guys that I dated loved me or had strong emotions towards me and I didn't have any towards them. It was just something to do to pass the time. Aimless dating.

My ex-boyfriend from Savannah reappeared into my life. I went home for the holidays to be with him and my family. He proposed to me. I said yes without thinking twice. I just wanted to be married. I went back to Miami after the trip and had a conversation with him about our living situation. He still didn't want to move to Miami, so I started looking for a job in Savannah. To save money for the wedding, I moved out of my apartment and moved in with an elderly family member while I continued searching for jobs in Savannah. For several months, he came down to visit me, and helped me plan for the wedding, until one day he called me and said that he was not going through with the marriage. Again, I trusted this man, and he let me down. He had no respect for my feelings and felt like he was able to come in and out of my life as he pleased. He tried to call me a few months later to say that he was ready to get married. Due to the hurt that I had been through with him, I told him it was too late. He then married someone else a few months later. I couldn't believe the news. Trying to make sense of how he could move on so quickly, I called him, and he professed his love to me and said that he only married his wife after I rejected him.

Like a fool, I believed him. A few months later, he told me he left her, and he moved to Miami to be with me. The truth always has a way of coming out and I found out that she was moving to Miami a few months later. He never left her. Ashamed to say, I allowed this back-and-forth chaos to continue for several years.

When I released myself from that mess, I quickly entered another relationship; this time with an older white man that I worked with. He treated me very well, bought me gifts all the time, and took care of me when I was sick. I felt wanted and appreciated, but he had his dark side as well. He was very jealous and felt that I was going to leave him for a younger black man all the time. This went on for three years and ended with me returning to my ex-fiancé. The drama between the two of them really drove me crazy. If I could have combined the good qualities of the both, I would have had the perfect man. It was at that time that I decided to leave Miami for another fresh start.

I moved to Columbia, SC in June 2001. I was over 30 and felt that it was time to get married! But, as always, I dated with no real feelings for anyone. I just wanted to be married not even realizing what that type of relationship and commitment required. I started to think back on all my encounters with men, and an image of my dad, Jimmie, kept revealing itself. I hated him. I made him invisible and tucked him away in a corner in my mind, but it was time to bring him out along with all the feelings I had towards him.

I felt that by this time in my life, he should have apologized to me for not being active in my life. I had accomplished a lot and never got a congratulations on graduating from high school, college, or graduate school and my birthdays were never acknowledged. It was at that point that I decided to seek counseling because I felt that my feelings towards Jimmie were causing the problems in my romantic relationships. I believed that my easy dismal from relationships was a result of me not wanting to be hurt by a man, and the choice of older men was based on looking for a protector and a provider.

I began counseling on my "daddy issues". My first assignment was to write down the feelings that I had towards Jimmie. My feelings included hostility, anger, disgust, and hatred. I described how every time that I saw him, my heart would get tight and I would get angry. By this time Jimmie was living with his mother in Savannah, and every time I came to visit, he had the nerve to ask me for money! Every conversation was him commenting on how I was making good money, had a nice car, and a house. After going to counseling for three months, my next assignment was to have a conversation with Jimmie in person.

While home for Christmas, we were all at my grandma's house. I asked Jimmie to take a ride with me. Everyone saw us walking out and they were shocked that we were leaving together. We ended up at Applebee's. I looked at him and asked why he never interacted with me or showed any love towards me. He sat there across from me and blamed it on the fact that I was always angry with him. I admitted it was true, but it was also because he always ignored me. He then opened up to me and told me about how at 17, he didn't know how to be a father and that before I was born, he moved back to Savannah. He admitted to putting me out of his mind and moving on with his life. He said that he knew his father, but also didn't have a relationship with him and didn't have any positive men in his life. He also talked about how he didn't make anything of himself as compared to his siblings and that he was the black sheep of the family because he was a result of an affair.

I told him that his treatment of women, drug use, jail/prison time, and his being absent in my life, affected my relationships with men. It was because I didn't want to date anyone like him a I would push away men who I thought tried to control me. I also told him how difficult it was for me to develop feelings of love because I always felt that they would eventually leave me just like he left me. So, I would always try to be the one to leave the relationship before giving a man the opportunity to leave me. He then said that he was sorry that his actions and behaviors caused me to have relationship problems and hoped that I would have a successful relationship because I deserved to be happy. We resolved to continue to work on our relationship by staying in touch and talking by phone on a regular basis.

I hoped that Jimmie and I could continue to work on our relationship, but that didn't happen. A fatherless man does not know how to be a father. Jimmie had minimal contact with his dad. This lack of contact made him feel less than a man. Growing up, I was able to see his lack of motivation and continued drug and alcohol use which resulted in repeated jail terms. I had to find it in myself to forgive him for not being a present father in my life due to this fact. That forgiveness released the weight I carried around regarding our non-relationship.

I learned to love myself. After having the discussion with Jimmie, I was able to begin working on myself. I became more confident and able to realize that I was worthy of love. I continued counseling and worked on my issues and insecurities. Throughout my life, I have had several relationships and two marriages that both have ended in divorce. I was finally able to accept my issues that led to these failed marriages, and how I lost myself chasing love and attention.

When I see Jimmie now, the only feelings that I have for him are sympathy because he has lived a life full of bad decisions. He is a broken man who has not made any attempts to improve the relationships with any of his four children. I am the only child who has made the decision to take out a life insurance policy and became his Health Care Power of Attorney so that he can be taken care of because I know that no one else will.

What I know for sure is that I have been greatly affected by being a fatherless daughter. I have learned that by speaking to Jimmie in person regarding my feelings, I was able to release the anger and hurt that had been with me my entire life. With the help of counseling, I was able to see how the hurt of being a fatherless daughter affected my personal and romantic relationships with men. Once I was able to put that baggage in the trash, I was able to have happy relationships without being so quick to end them when I didn't like certain aspects. It taught me how to communicate my feelings in a positive way, and I am now a happy, confident woman who is finally at peace in her life.

The Impact of Tonya's Story on Your Life

What moment in this story resonated with you the most?

____

____

____

____

____

____

How has this story impacted you?

____

____

____

____

____

____

Tonya Hart

Early in life, a near fatal car accident resulted in her having two broken legs, a broken pelvis and broken arm and being in a body cast for three months. Although physically broken and immobile at 3 years of age, Tonya's Spirit and Will were still soaring.

Today, Tonya is a Resilient Woman of Purpose whose mission is to heal hearts, transform minds and show others in spite of their circumstances, destiny awaits!

Tonya graduated from Savannah State University with a Bachelor's Degree in Social Work and then earned a Master's Degree in Social Work from Florida State University.

Tonya has been employed with the VA Medical Center for 24 years with 17 at the Columbia, SC VA Medical Center where she serves Veterans with Spinal Cord Injuries, Multiple Sclerosis, and ALS.

Tonya's goal is to Empower women and girls by sharing her story of overcoming many challenges in hopes that they will be able to live their Best Lives!

Tonya has been a member of Alpha Kappa Alpha, Sorority Inc. for 27 years; is a member of the SC Team of The National Kidney

Foundation; and serves as the Treasurer for the Columbia Association of the National Association of Black Social Workers. Tonya is a member of Brookland Baptist Church Northeast.

CHAPTER FIVE

MY FEAR OF FATHERLESSNESS

Ebony Looney

For most of my life I was raised by my mother and moved frequently from Columbia, SC to Charlotte, NC, to New York City. My father was only around during my early years when I was too young to remember. With each passing year, I grew curious about this man. *What did he look like? Why did he leave? Was he still alive?* One day I approached my mother and asked about him. She was vague, and I could tell she was uncomfortable with the conversation.

"Why do you need to know, now?" She asked.

I remained silent.

"You're doing fine. I made the decision to raise you alone. I didn't need anyone. And it was all so long ago anyway," she continued didn't say much back then. I later thought about what she said and concluded that she in fact was right. I am doing just fine without a father. I also had other men in my life who were like father figures to me. They were there to give me advice when I needed it. They filled that daddy void.

In 2002, I saw the movie, *Antwone Fisher*, and the desire to know my father awakened. In the movie, the main character Antoine

Fisher, who was dealing with anger issue at his job, was encouraged to deal with his past. As a child who grew up in foster care, he had several unfortunate things happen to him. On his journey to finding who he really was, he asked his foster mother about his biological family. This led him to finding his biological mother who was a struggling drug addict.

That was the first scene in the movie that hit close to home for me. Over the years, I watched as my mother struggled with drug addictions herself. She did the best she could, but I knew that addictions had the power to make things in life extremely complicated.

After meeting his biological mother, Antwone Fisher was also led to the rest of his biological family. They prepared a huge dinner and family reunion as they welcomed him into their lives and said, "We are your family."

Tears flowed on the screen and on my cheeks. Ugly cry and all, I was captivated by this movie. I desperately wanted that "we are your people; let's eat" kind of moment too. I approached my mother again with the same question.

"Who is my father? Are you sure you don't have any information on him?"

She sighed and told me which city he lived in, but she wasn't exactly sure where he was at the moment because it had been years since she last spoke to him.

With the information she gave me, I was determined to find my father like Antwone Fisher found his family. I used the phone book to research possible leads, but apparently, the list of men who had my father's first and last name was much longer than I had expected.

Still, I was eager to find my Hollywood ending. I sat down and made my first call.

"Hello, my name is Ebony. Is there a James there by chance?

"Who is his and why? The person responded hesitantly.

"Um, I was just wondering if you knew my mother... I'm her daughter, Ebony, and um, James might be my daddy."

There was an awkward silence.

"Um, no. Wrong number."

I repeated this for several calls, each one sounding similar in tone and filled with such awkward feelings. I couldn't believe that I had to cold-call to try and find this person who helped create me. I hated cold calling. I used to work a sales job and quit after two weeks of cold calling. Having to call a complete stranger to say, "Hey, I think you might be my daddy," was even more terrifying than asking for someone to buy shoes or insurance.

The list of names overwhelmed me, and I convinced myself that maybe it really didn't matter. Besides, I was doing fine without him. I had just married the love of my life, and he was going to be my protector. Over time, I learned to let it go. The idea of being graciously received by him with a huge dinner and with additional family members seemed nice, but it might not ever happen. From time to time I still wonder who he is. I wonder what his family is like, and whenever I meet people with the same maiden name as me, I can't help but to inquire about if they have a James in their family.

I still hold on to the hope that one day maybe I'll find them accidentally, without trying. Until then, I will go on with my life and look on the brighter side of things. I'm grateful for who I have, and the fact that they always make me feel like I belong.

I also learned that it was ok for me to move on with my life. This survival and defense mechanism, I believe, has helped me push through as an entrepreneur. I use what I have to get the job done. I have encouraged other young women to use their skills and abilities to problem solve their way out of an issue.

I have learned to be self-sufficient. I am capable of taking care of myself. However, as a married woman, I am now working on balancing this independent thinking so that I can allow my husband to take care of me.

The Impact of Ebony's Story on Your Life

What moment in this story resonated with you the most?

____

____

____

____

____

____

How has this story impacted you?

____

____

____

____

____

____

Ebony Looney

Ebony Looney is the founder and CEO of Make Me Over, EB. She helps entrepreneurs build, brand and run their business with ease, grace and style. Ebony's enthusiastic hands-on interactive approach will delight audiences of any organization looking to educate, inspire and provide a little

fun! She has been invited as a guest speaker for organizations, non-profits, colleges, universities, women's groups and small businesses with anywhere between 20 and 200 attendees. Past clients have included: Claflin University, Benedict College, Richland County Public Library, Office of Business Opportunity (City of Columbia), Engenuity (Lower Richland High School). She has over 15 years experience in image consulting, marketing, web development, and blogging.

CHAPTER SIX

GRACE FOR DADDY

Cynthia Rhue Hillian

I had the best kindergarten teacher ever... Ms. Cribb. She looked exactly like the grandmother that owned Tweetie Bird in The Looney Tunes. She smelled like cookies and had great big apron pockets that were always filled with something to make me feel better. Kindergarten was my safe place. Ms. Cribb had the biggest, softest, warmest lap in the world. Laying on her lap was like falling into a deep bath of liquid love.

Because of my birthday being in January, I was able to be with Ms. Cribb for two years. In her classroom, I felt peace and security. When I turned seven, I was removed from my place of safety as I entered first grade without her.

Home life was far from perfect. When Mama used to leave the house to run errands or go to work, I hated it. Things would happen when she wasn't around. My brother and I were trained to be very quiet because the noise always annoyed Daddy. He was 20 years older than Mama, he yelled a lot, and he always threatened to beat us. On most days he refrained from hitting me for some reason. But one day, while Mama was out taking Grandmama and Granddaddy to their doctor's appointments in the neighboring city, Daddy lost his patience with me. Mama found me unconscious on the floor with my dress all tattered. Mama threatened him that if he ever did something like that again, she would call the sheriff. After that incident, when my brother and I were left with him, I would hide in my closet and play with my dolls until Mama came home.

I never understood why he was so angry. We tried our best to make the least amount of noise possible. He and Mama used to get into arguments all the time; there was never a moment of peace in our home. It was days like that, when they threatened to hit each other, that I would think back about my safe place, Ms. Cribbs classroom.

There were some days he did nice things, and that would make it harder for me to know exactly how I should feel about him. I hated the way he treated our family, but I loved when he took the time to teach me something, like the time he taught me to look under dead logs for worms because he knew how much I loved playing with them. I learned during those moments of seeing every side to him that it was okay to like him, but dangerous to love him.

During that time, I began to talk to God. I had so many questions, yet no answers. Someone once told me that God was everywhere, and that He was always watching over us. But I wondered how that was even possible. How could God with his infinite power and wisdom leave me with a family like this? I felt like it was all a mistake, and I continued to pray for answers.

Maya Angelou has a quote that says, "When people know better, they do better." Well, maybe that was just it. He didn't know any better. He tried to do what he knew how to do. He provided for our basic needs, but he didn't know how to connect with us on an emotional level. He had trauma with his own father which caused him to be a troubled man.

The messages we receive and the patterns we create from those messages as small children seem to serve us well in that moment. You see, hating daddy felt like the neutral zone to keep the peace with Mama. Hiding in the closet while she was gone served me then. But then I noticed I was still hiding, long after the closet was gone.

A few years later, Daddy ended up in the intensive care unit at the Medical University. For four months, Mama and I would drive up the road to visit him every day, uncertain about what was going to happen to him. He requested to be taken off the ventilator and to be placed on oxygen, and over the next several days he became a different person. On his strong days, he tried to start conversations with me and it made me feel softer towards him. One night while I was at home, the phone rang, and it was him. His tone was unfamiliar, it was full of happiness and joy. He called to say that he asked God for forgiveness, and he also asked Mama for hers. He was sorry for not knowing any better. He thanked me for teaching him how to pray and read the Bible. I didn't even know I had taught him that, but I guess he did see me throughout all those years, even though I felt like I was invisible.

The next day, when Mama and I arrived at the house, it was dusk dark. We had long since moved from the country and we had neighbors. Mrs. Kelly, our nearest neighbor, had brought in the clothes that were on the line for us. Mama stopped on the stoop and chatted with her while I excused myself and went on in the house and sat in the big chair in front of the television. Thinking about the events of the day and thinking I needed to get Mama in the house so she could eat something, the telephone rang. I answered. It was the Medical University ICU nurse. Daddy was gone.

Even though he was physically there my entire life, I never really had a relationship with him. Those last few months while he was in ICU were the only moments we actually had great conversations. Those were moments when I was able to see him as a human being, as a father, and have compassion towards him.

Here is what I know. I know that love, understanding, and forgiveness are powerful forces for change. I know that love covers and heals. I know a lot of things, hidden things, hard things, things that have been revealed now, that my seven-year-old self was always asking about, could not have been fathomed. I was being protected. And no, things are not always as they seem. Some things we may never know. It is very important to know that hurt people, hurt other people. My daddy had a story. I was just a part of it. A story that was sometimes too painful to share. He did not get it all right, but I believe God gave him the grace to try.

The Impact of Cynthia's Story on Your Life

What moment in this story resonated with you the most?

____

____

____

____

____

____

How has this story impacted you?

____

____

____

____

____

____

____

Cynthia Rhue Hillian

Cynthia is from the Low Country of South Carolina. She enjoyed many years working as a medical professional. She currently spends a lot of her time studying alternative healing modalities. She loves relaxing and spending time with her husband near the ocean. Cynthia also enjoys reading a good book, writing in her journal and will be launching her new project, a Blog for women who are challenged with their foundational primary relationships.

CHAPTER SEVEN

THROUGH THE EYES OF A CHILD

Vanessa Guyton

I was awakened in the middle of the night by the sounds of my mother crying, whimpering, and trying to breathe. At approximately four years of age, I remember tiptoeing downstairs to see why my mother was crying and why my dad was yelling "Shut Up." Once I made it down the wooden stairs, I saw my mother sitting on the floor, laying her head up against the white brick wall in our living room. I saw tears running down her dark skin, and her long hair in a disarray. As I write this, I am not even sure if they realized that I was watching, or as my grandmother would say, "being nosey". I don't remember much of that night, but I do know that it wasn't the last time I would witness my dad abusing my mother and experiencing events that would have a lasting impact on all of my future relationships.

My dad was a Soldier in the United States Army. I thought he was strong, smart, and handsome in his green fatigues. I can remember waiting outside on the porch to see what special gift he had for me. He was my natural protector and treated me like the son he never had. I was girlie, yet rough. I wanted to be just like him. I even stole his cigarettes and tried to emulate his every move. Well, that was until he caught me with his cigarettes and taught me a life-long lesson of never inhaling. My dad was my everything. I wanted to marry a man just like him. This is why I couldn't understand how he could be so sweet one day and downright mean the next.

My parents were high school sweethearts. My mother became pregnant and my dad did the honorable thing by marrying her and joining the Army to take care of his family. They both experienced very difficult childhoods. My dad never met his dad until he was 17, and his mother died when he was 9. My mother came from a very large family where her dad was very abusive to her mom until the day he died. Neither one of them knew what a healthy marriage or relationship looked like. No one taught them how to love or how to express their emotions. This obviously led to two people looking to each other for the love they never experienced or witnessed. Essentially, two broken teenagers, coming together to continue the generational pattern of hurt.

Years would pass, and my mother would silently endure being abused by the man that we both loved. Even when she considered leaving, her mother advised her to stay because she had a "good man" and she believed in marriage until death do you part—regardless of the abuse. She was an isolated stay-at-home mom, with three daughters, and very few friends who weren't experiencing the same acts of abuse in their home. How do you report abuse when your husband financially supports you and your children? During that time, the military was a network of "good ole boys." My dad was an exceptional soldier so, essentially, he was untouchable. However, this changed once the Military Police visited our home one too many times. His Commander instructed him to make a decision...Choose between your Army career or your family. Sadly, he chose his Army career and divorced my mom when I was nine. (This information I found out from my dad 20 years later.)

I didn't understand divorce or why we moved back to Florida with my Aunt and her family. It was like it was a big secret that couldn't be explained. Now that I look back, maybe I didn't want to understand and was in denial about my family. We went from being a middle-class military family, to a poor family eventually living in the infamous projects in between Winter Park and Eatonville called Chocolate City. I began to hate the soldier that I so passionately called daddy. I hated that he hurt my mom; I hated that he left us; I hated that he traveled all over the world being the "Perfect Soldier" and only came home once or twice a year.

I became distant and I made mediocre grades. Now that I look back, and understand depression, I realize that I suffered from it in my preteen years. I isolated myself in a fantasy world of books and romance novels. I thought that I would find answers to my questions in books. Why would a man leave his family when he was supposed to love them and provide for them? Why would a man intentionally hurt you and make you cry? In my mind, when a man left his family, he no longer loved them. I longed to be loved again, to wait patiently for my dad to come home. I longed to have the life like the women in the Harlequin Romance novels.

I didn't realize until 30 years later, that the love that I was missing from my father caused so many problems in my life. My self-esteem was very low and I didn't think that I was worthy of love because my dad no longer loved me. This led to me losing my virginity at an early age, because I wanted someone to love me and make me feel special like my dad used to make me feel. After feeling that all men were the same, and only wanted sex, and becoming a teenage mother, I made a drastic change in my life. I became very mean to men, and dared one to hit me, more-less raise their voice at me. I refused to let a man get close enough to me to ever abuse me or even to love me because of my fear of another man leaving me. I had serious trust issues and didn't believe that a man could be faithful or truly love me. I even stopped speaking to my dad because I was filled with hurt and rage about my life. I blamed him for everything that went wrong in my life, including being poor and living in the projects. Needless to say, men didn't have a chance in my world. I became focused on my daughter and our future.

Deep down, I still loved my dad and respected him for serving his country. Instead of going to college, I joined the Army, immediately after high school. I had always wanted to be like my dad. Now I wore the same uniform he wore and honorably served the same country as he did. We were even both stationed together in Germany for a year. I had started speaking to him again because I wanted him in my daughter's life. But I didn't truly forgive him, and I still blamed him for the unhappiness in my life.

While living in Germany, I met a man, who complimented me every day. He was tall, handsome, with a crooked smile that would melt your heart and make you feel all warm inside. His name was Tony, a "High-Speed Soldier" and a ladies' man, very similar to my dad. I initially ignored him for months, because he reminded me of my dad, but it was also the same reason I started to pay attention to him. One day, after months of ignoring him, I finally allowed him to take me out on a date. He was very charismatic and vowed to love me and give me the world. I married my best friend and at first everything was perfect. We became a blended family and had another child together.

Somehow all of my insecurities about love and trust became evident in my marriage. I never allowed him to be the head of our family and take true control of the decisions in our marriage and I always had a fear that he would hurt me. The emotions from my childhood were still there. We survived over 20 years of marriage, but it was tough. I pushed him away on many occasions and never trusted him when he left the house. Some of the mistrust was due to some of his actions and also my childhood experiences. Eventually, my marriage failed for multiple reasons, but I do accept some fault in that I did not deal with my childhood baggage. Today, he is still my friend and I will always cherish every moment that I have him in my life.

Now at the age of 42, I am finally able to reflect on the emotional baggage I have been carrying around since childhood. I started by talking with a counselor, journaling, acknowledging the real problem, forgiving my dad, and forgiving myself.

Over the years I have seen approximately 70 counselors. I didn't remain in counseling for various reasons, to include not trusting my counselors. I kept searching until I found someone that I trusted and could open up my heart to. She changed my life. We started talking about my life as a child, and how I really didn't understand relationships or knew what was going on between my parents. I made assumptions and created a world that was not necessarily true. I told myself that my dad did not love his family and I believed that he was perfect and would not make mistakes. Can you imagine how I felt after realizing that she was absolutely RIGHT? I had envisioned a fantasy life, like the lives of the characters in the books I read. How could I expect my dad to be perfect when he didn't even have an example of a perfect man? How could I blame him for everything, when I really didn't understand my mother and her example of how a man should treat a woman? How would I feel if my children blamed me for every bad thing that happened in my marriage that eventually failed?

After finally reaching a major break-through with my counselor, we discussed journaling my thoughts and feelings. I started writing about my mom and her experiences before and after marriage. I tried to understand how my mom felt and the journey she experienced, and I was able to understand so much more about her. I acknowledged her strengths and the sacrifices she made for her daughters. I journaled about my dad and I was able to find peace and clarity about a journey that was different from novels. I journaled about my children and the decisions that I made that may have affected them. Last but not least, I journaled about my marriage and things that went wrong and right, and the role I played that was not always positive. I journal daily, and it has helped me tremendously. I feel like once you put it on paper, it becomes your reality and truth. You have to decide what you are going to do with your thoughts and your future.

Acknowledging the good and bad about your life, and the fact that it has become a problem that has affected you to your core, is a major key to moving forward. I had to acknowledge that my childhood was still affecting my adult life and decisions. I had to acknowledge that my life did "stink" and that I wasn't perfect. I had to acknowledge that my imagination was vivid and created an unrealistic life. I had to acknowledge that my husband and other men that I was with were mistreated because of my life experiences that occurred before them. I had to acknowledge that I have a lot of work to do to heal my heart and soul.

Forgiving my dad was one of the most challenging things that I have ever done in my life!! I had to forgive a man for abusing my mother, divorcing his family, and for removing our standard of living. How do you truly forgive your dad? You forgive by realizing that there is no manual or guideline to being a parent. They will make mistakes, especially if they didn't have a good example. I know my dad loves me, but sometimes it's hard to love when you never felt love. I have completely forgiven my dad. This has allowed us to be the best of friends. I am finally at a point that I can enjoy his company and talk about everything from football to money. I had to realize that I couldn't make up the time we lost, but to cherish the time that we have left.

I had to forgive myself for all of the mistakes I have made in life. I couldn't keep blaming it on my childhood. I had to accept responsibilities for my actions and realize that I made some bad choices, and that it was time to learn from them and move forward. Then I had to acknowledge that, I was created by God and he didn't make any mistakes. The journey I lived was for me to create experiences that will allow me to help others and to be a better woman. I am not perfect, but I am a good woman and I will always embrace that thought.

I am so thankful, because now, I have an awesome relationship with my dad who is 62. I enjoy spending time with him and listening to his Army stories and I even call him for advice. He has learned from his mistakes and has become a better man, dad, and granddad. When we finally had a real conversation about my childhood, it gave him the opportunity to explain to me the variables in his life that I didn't know about. Unknowingly, I had made a lot of assumptions about my dad and my parent's marriage. This conversation also gave me the opportunity to tell him how I really felt and how living in a home with domestic violence affected my life. Having a candid conversation changed both of our lives and allowed us to heal.

I have learned from my dad, that regardless of the circumstances or mistakes in life that occur, we can always learn from them and be better than we were yesterday. Realizing that my dad and mother truly love me, allows me to truly love myself and to believe that I deserve to be loved. I am still working on myself, but now I am able to go into a new relationship without my childhood baggage and with an optimistic look on life.

The Impact of Vanessa's Story on Your Life

What moment in this story resonated with you the most?

____

____

____

____

____

____

How has this story impacted you?

____

____

____

____

____

____

Dr. Vanessa L. Guyton

Dr. Vanessa L. Guyton is the CEO of Consulting Experts & Associates, LLC. CEA is a global training consulting firm that assists organizations in improving training and organization effectiveness. Dr. Guyton honorably served in the United States Army as a Human Resource Manager for 10 years. Additionally, she is a credentialed Victim Advocate and has certified over 3,200 Sexual Assault Response Coordinators and Victim Advocates. Her training is provided globally to thousands of military organizations, colleges, and corporations on The Hush Topics: sexual assault, sexual harassment, drug facilitated sexual assault, LGQBT sexual assault, disabled victims, sex trafficking, suicide prevention, domestic violence, bystander intervention, and refresher training. She is also the founder of Victorious, a non-profit organization that provides support for victims as they transition. Dr. Guyton was appointed by the National Organization for Victim Assistance (NOVA) as an Advisory Board Member for the National Advocacy Leadership Center in 2015.

CHAPTER EIGHT

BECOMING A FATHERLESS DAUGHTER

Brenda French

I guess you could say I've always been a fatherless daughter. There was no difference in our interactions between the time my dad was living at home to when he finally decided to move out. My day-to-day routine never included him. He just wasn't that into me. It seemed like everything else outside of our home held more value than my mother and I. And little did we know that he was in the process of creating a new family. We received the news that his mistress became pregnant. Ironically, she had the same name as me, and I wondered how he could be out with her, saying her name, and never feeling an ounce of guilt or shame.

He carried on his affair for several years; moving in and out of our home when things went bad with her. Eventually, he asked my mother for a divorce and told her that he just didn't want to be tied down anymore. I guess he just didn't want to be tied down to us because not even five months later, he was married to someone else and awaiting his long-coveted son. His namesake. Along with that new marriage, he became a stepfather to two little girls. I didn't know much about them, but it was truly apparent how much he adored them.

While he was enjoying his new family, my mother and I were left with feelings of rejection and unworthiness. There was no longer room for me in his life.

My mother and I tried to make the most out of our circumstances. We had a house in foreclosure, a broken down pickup truck that was in need of a new engine, and a house filled with furniture that was donated from the church. My mother was trying her best to make ends meet. She was a high school dropout with a minimum-wage job that left us no choice but to move to a cheap apartment in a rough neighborhood. We had two dogs at the time that we truly loved, but unfortunately, they were not allowed in the new apartment. My father agreed to care for them, but instead, dumped them in a boarding facility and gave them my mother's information as the contact to place on file. Because of his unreliability, we had to take the dogs to a shelter, and I never saw them again. He would always say one thing and then do another, and this made me feel like I just wasn't important to him at all. He wasn't concerned about me. He wasn't concerned about where or how I was going to live.

He played this game where he was in and out of my life throughout my school years. I felt like I was traded for an upgrade, his three new children. He never offered to help my mother provide for my financial needs so, she had to continually take him to court for child support. This caused me to develop such distrust towards people in general. If my own father could continuously lie to me and break promises, then how in the world could I expect anything more from anyone else?

As I was considering whether or not to go to college, I brought up the conversation to my father. He told me that I should indeed attend and that he would pay for everything. I thought to myself, *Wow! My dad is rich!* With the $50 I had in my pocket, I applied to one college and was accepted. A few months later, I was living in the dorms, taking classes, and making good grades. After I sent him the bill for my second semester, he told me that he couldn't pay for it after all. It was too expensive. I was faced with financial expulsion from the university. If it wasn't for the parents of a friend of mine giving me the funds for the second semester, I have no idea where I would be right now. Without my dad's help, I graduated with my Bachelor's degree in Accounting.

Over the next several years, I tried to block him out of my mind and life. There was still a part of me that wanted to at least know if he was still alive so, I would check the obituaries from time to time to see if I ever came across his name. 12 years passed without me seeing or hearing from him. By that time, I was a licensed CPA, started my own public accounting practice, and was in a solid, happy marriage.

Facebook came along and the first thing I did was look up my paternal cousins. They were some of my most favorite people. We were all so happy to talk to each other after 23 years!

Coincidentally, my aunt and uncle happened to be in Denver visiting my father and brother at the time. They quickly set up a reunion at my brother's house for the following weekend. I was in no way ready for that. All along, I was really only interested in keeping in touch with my cousins. Surprisingly, the reunion was an amazing thing! My pain and resentment fell away and I thought that I was finally going to have my family back. We all took a trip to Canada together and I was on top of the world. I didn't want it to end. It did though. Within three years, my father lost interest again. He stopped calling. My greeting cards were not returned. My phone messages were not returned. The last time I spoke to him on the phone for Father's Day, he had such an ugly tone in his voice. The call lasted just a couple of minutes, and I never heard from him again.

Last year, my mom was diagnosed with pulmonary fibrosis. She was told that it would be fatal within three to five years. I was devastated. I figured she was going to live at least as long as I had. She had to, right? Besides my husband, she is my only family. As she journeyed through the phases of grief, I became increasingly overwhelmed by it all. I needed someone to listen to me and really hear me. I had hoped that I could lean on my brother since we had been reconnecting in such positive ways. But early one Saturday morning in April, I received a text from him that read, *Stop fucking sending me texts like this.* I was hurt and confused. I cried for days while finishing up my tax season.

I tried to rationalize it. *Maybe he was hacked? Maybe he was sleep-walking?* We never spoke again.

So, I took to pouring out my soul on Facebook. This brought telephone calls from both my cousin and my aunt, neither of whom I had spoken to in years. As I spoke to them about what was going on, I couldn't help but to ask about my father. I went on asking them questions like, *Why does he hate me so much? Why won't he talk to me? What did I do?* Neither of them could explain it nor understand it. But they both told me the exact same thing. *We don't want to say anything to him because then he might stop talking to us too.* Those words spoke to me loud and clear. I was not important enough. Then another cousin told me that I needed mental help and needed it right away, so she sent me the link for shrinks in my area.

After losing a few nights of sleep, I finally decided that I needed to protect my peace. I couldn't keep pretending with these people that everything was OK. It wasn't OK. I knew that they were not going to go to bat for me, so I cut ties. It was too painful to see pictures of my father on Facebook enjoying his family in Canada when he only lived 45 minutes away from me and never saw me. It was too painful to see photos of my niece and nephews knowing that I would never have a relationship with them. No matter how hard I tried, I was an outsider. I needed to move on with my life, and so I did. I decided that I would never again let them into my circle.

I then started to do some soul searching and read my first book on Fatherless Daughters. I was immediately uplifted. I was not alone after all. I discovered that there are millions of women across the globe that grew up in similar situations as mine. But they found hope within a group of special women. So, I searched for a group on Facebook and found one. Then shortly thereafter I found a Christian radio station that spoke to me. I began listening to it every day. I started studying the Bible again and renewing my relationship with Christ.

Through my healing journey, I was able to recognize the shared characteristics I had with other fatherless women. We are often driven to success, while at the same time, struggle in our relationships with people and with money. I had a tough time forming positive relationships with men. I could not handle male authority while I was in school. I would cause trouble in my classes with male teachers. I rebelled in many ways. I experimented with drugs and alcohol. I was a little too loose in my feeble search for a boyfriend and was always left feeling ugly and ashamed. To this day, I do not do well with male authority in the workplace. So much so, I started my own business to get away from it.

I did not have any children of my own because of the pain my father caused me. I didn't feel like I had anything to offer a child, because I still felt like one in many ways. I could envision myself as a neglectful mother, so I just didn't do it. During college when

I was dating my future husband, I began to push him away every so often so that I would not be the one who was left...just in case he was thinking of dumping me. This behavior continued well into my 30's.

I know that I have something to teach young girls and boys in similar situations. I have been volunteering for a large charitable organization at the high school level assisting kids who are getting ready to graduate and move on from high school. These kids are all disadvantaged in some way; whether it's with finances, family life, or language barriers. It's a learning experience for me as well. I now understand that I am far from alone and that I am a worthy individual who deserves the best that life has to offer. And I will continue to make it a priority to let other girls and boys know that they deserve the same.

The Impact of Brenda's Story on Your Life

What moment in this story resonated with you the most?

____

____

____

____

____

____

How has this story impacted you?

____

____

____

____

____

____

Brenda French

Brenda French is a 50 year old Colorado native and has been married for 26 years. She's a self-employed CPA and have been in the industry for 23 years. Brenda describes herself as childfree,but she's is loving mother to two furry kids, Duke and Bella. She love learning, crafting/sewing, and taking RV trips with our dogs.

CHAPTER NINE

FATHERLESS WITH OUR FATHER

Jean Harrison

We are overcome by the words of our testimony, so here it goes. My first memories of my family are awesome. I have three sisters and three brothers and we were very close. We played together in our large back yard for hours. My mother was a stay-at-home mom, but she ran a tight ship. She cooked, cleaned, washed clothes, but she always knew when we were getting into something. During the week my father worked two jobs, but the weekends would be filled with all kinds of adventures. Sometimes we would all pack up into our Sunday Rider, which was a shiny black Buick with shiny rims and custom-made bubble plastic seat covers. We all loved to ride in the Buick. I would sit in the front seat right next to my daddy and my little brother was next to me with my mother beside him. I felt so safe and happy. To me there was nothing better.

Our adventures could lead us up at the zoo in Charleston, or we would go to the airport and watch the planes jet in and take off. Every year we would go to the beach and we would visit Six Flags in Georgia. On Sundays there was always church, and we had our weekly visits with our grandparents. I loved Sunday evenings as we would all sit around the TV and watch Bonanza and eat ice cream. But before we started our Sunday ritual, my daddy would sit in his big chair and wait for me to climb up on his lap and ask for ice cream. And then he would say "if my baby girl wants ice cream, we will have ice cream". Then he would jump up and give us all ice cream. I was a daddy's girl. I was his "baby girl" and when he called me that it made my heart leap with joy. My daddy always made me feel special and loved.

During the week my father got home from work around 11:00 pm and once or twice during the week my father would bring home three large cheeseburgers. My mother would cut two of the cheeseburgers into four pieces and wake all of us up to receive our portion. It would be such a treat for us. Life was so good. To me it couldn't get any better. My daddy made sure we had everything we needed and many things that we wanted. He would buy us a new pool every year. It would be so tall that I could not get in without one of my siblings lifting me over the wall of the pool. Whenever one of my siblings wanted something, they would tell me to ask my father, because they were assured that he would get it for me. I don't ever remember my daddy telling me no to anything. I felt so special and important.

Yes, life was really, really good. I remember him giving my mom money for our school clothes and I would get to pick any shoes that I wanted. I would be overjoyed and I could not wait for school to start. My mom and dad would attend all of our school programs and encourage us to be involved. My dad would drill my older sisters and brothers with their time tables. My parents did not like C's on our report cards and if anyone of us would venture into bring home anything less, my father would surely make us regret it.

When I was 7 years old I could feel that things were changing between my mom and dad. I would be awakened at night now, not for a hamburger, but because of arguing. It would be my mom's voice that would cut into my sound sleep at night. I couldn't understand what was being said or why my mom was angry with my dad, but I knew that it wasn't a good thing. I knew better than to ask about it. My body would begin to shake in fear and I would cry myself back to sleep most nights. But the next day, everything would return to normal and all was well until the next time. Things escalated and the arguing became more frequent. I remember one night it got so bad that my brother got in between Mom and Dad and calmed them down.

It was the spring of my third-grade year that life as I knew it changed forever. On that dreaded day my siblings and I were lined up from the oldest to the youngest. Mom and Dad started with the oldest and asked each one what we thought they should do, continue to stay together or have Dad leave. Not one of my older siblings wanted my daddy to stay. They all wanted the arguing to stop. My heart was beating so fast by the time they got to me that I could barely breathe. I managed to scream, "Noooooo, I don't want my daddy to leave." I cried so hard that

I had to be removed from the room by my sister. My heart was broken. The decision was made, and my father had to leave. He got down on his knee in front of me and grabbed my shoulders and promised me that he would visit so often that I wouldn't even know that he was gone. Then he gave me the biggest hug ever and I sank my face into his shoulder and sobbed quietly. Then he was gone.

My father did visit us frequently the first two months or so. After that the visits became less frequent and by the fifth month all contact ended. My life had changed so drastically and so suddenly that my mind would not or could not accept what was happening. I shut down and became really quiet. I did not want to go to school and I tried to tell my mom that I was not feeling well. She immediately took my temperature and it was normal. She told me that I would be alright and sent me off to school. I fell into a depression and my self-esteem went down drastically. I felt that I was no longer a complete person, I felt that I was substandard. It was hard because all of the families that I knew in my neighborhood had fathers in their home. My thoughts were that something was wrong with me because my daddy left me and I had no clue as to why. It hurt so badly in the beginning because I totally loved my daddy and I thought he loved me, too. How could he leave me? Who would take me to the airport to watch the planes? Who would take me to the zoo? Whose lap would I climb onto on Sunday evening and ask for ice cream? Who daddy, who? I never cried after the visits stopped because

I felt that if I let the tears start, I would never be able to make them stop. The pain consumed me for the first few weeks and I began to put up walls in my heart just to be able to make it through the days.

My focus shifted toward my brothers. I prayed that they would be alright because I knew how much they needed Dad. How must they feel being boys and not having their father there for them? My dad would help my brothers get ready for church on Sundays. He would line them up and brush their hair and he would stand in the doorway and lean on the door with his arms folded and watch them brush their teeth. Sundays were very hard for me. Sunday, the day of the week that was filled with so much happiness is now sad and dark. I would now see my brothers rushing around to get themselves ready for church.

My dad was a mechanic and whenever he would work on cars, he would have my brothers right by his side handing him the tools. He would explain everything to them that he was doing to the cars. Every other weekend while my mom would take us to get our hair done, my dad would take the boys to the barber shop for haircuts. Who would now teach them the things they needed to know? Who would take them to the barber shop? How would my younger brother learn what my older brothers already knew about cars? Although I closely watched my brothers, my younger brother concerned me the most. I would ask God to send him someone to teach him all that he would need to know.

Focusing on my brothers and watching them closely took my mind away from my own pain. God answered the prayers and sent one of my neighbors to take my younger brother under his wing. He would take my little brother fishing, to ball games, and taught him to ride his bike. He would let my brother hang out with him and his son every day. This gave me a little peace of mind. I prayed that God would protect my brothers and give them what they needed.

My mother was a housewife up until my daddy left. She had to find a job, having never worked a day in her life. She got a job as a janitor. She worked very hard and I remember her coming home in the evenings and she was so tired. She would check over all of our homework. My older siblings would have dinner ready when she got home from work. My mom always worked hard and provided us with the things that we needed. We did not have a lot of fancy things, but she made sure that we had all of the necessities and sometimes some of the things we wanted. She taught me to be respectful, and kind to everyone.

Being a single mother of seven was not fair to her, and I saw it take a toll on her in the beginning. She was promised a husband to love her and take care of her. We were my father's children yes, but she was his wife. He was supposed to take care of her most of all, and it made me angry to have to see my mother struggle alone for so many years. However, I never heard her complain or say anything negative about my father. I know that had she told me the things that he did when I was younger, it would have made me angrier and I would have hated my father even more for leaving us. She would always tell us, "he is still your father, no matter what and you should check on him." I thank God for blessing me with such a wise and loving mother. Even though I was angry with my father for making my mother work so hard, I prayed for God to keep him safe, because I still loved him so.

I remember the feeling of being different, and less than the other children in the neighborhood, because everyone else had their fathers in the home. I felt like there was something wrong with me if my daddy would leave me. It always made me sad, so I would keep myself busy with my school work. I would read books but I would never choose books with families in them. I became shy and withdrawn and would just want to be invisible at school. In fifth grade, I was allowed to go over to my best friend's house. I loved her, but I stopped going because I was literally afraid of her father. He wasn't mean, he was actually kind and loving, but I didn't know how to respond to an adult man since I hadn't had my daddy in my life for two years. How I relate to older men only got worse over the years. Whenever I would have a male teacher, I would struggle to even say anything to them. I couldn't even answer questions in class. As a grown woman, I found it hard to hug men at church, who I considered to be my brothers. I had to learn to push past the desire to pull away. It was hard, but I learned to do it even though I actually hated it. Not knowing at the time why I could not reach out to my brothers, I knew something was not right about this.

Middle school was horrible for me. I was so closed off from everyone and everything except schoolwork. I had one friend that I would go to the park with and visit her house, but she had other friends that I wanted nothing to do with because my self-esteem was very low. Boys were beginning to get interested in girls at this age, but I was not interested because I did not want to be abandoned. I felt that boys, like my father, would show that they loved me and then leave me. I would rather be left alone by males. I was really quite mean to every boy that tried to even talk to me. I would not talk to them and if they got up the nerve to tell me that they liked me, I would tell them rudely to leave me alone. My face would tell the story. Do not bother me guys. I went to school because I had to do my school work, and that is all.

When I was in the seventh grade a boy asked me to be his girlfriend and I really liked him. I thought he was cute and funny. However, I was not going to give him the opportunity to hurt me, so I yelled, 'No' so loud at him that he never said anything to me again. And even though I liked him it was just fine with me that he totally left me alone. We had an eighth grade prom and I wanted to go, but everyone was taking a date, so I decided not to go. One of my classmates that I really had a secret crush on, got up the nerve to ask me to the dance. I quickly told him 'no' even though I really wanted to go. My best friend wanted me to go so bad, so she found me a date and begged me to come with her. She told me that all I had to do was go with him and I didn't have to hang around with him. Because I wanted to go, I said ok. When my friend's mom came to pick me up, she had already picked up our dates, but I would not sit next to my date in the car. When we arrived at the dance I totally ignored my date. I actually took pictures with an older boy that I barely knew, because he quietly begged me to take a picture with him. I was very rude to my date by ignoring him and I still regret that because he was a really nice, smart guy that did not deserve to be treated that way. I had become cold toward males and I wasn't even out of middle school.

High school years without my father were no better. As my ninth grade school year started, I went to a dance at school with a few of my friends. After the dance we caught a ride home with one of the older boys that we usually rode home with. This night, my friends were dropped off first and I was the last one to be dropped off. Instead of taking me home he drove to a dark spot near my home and he raped me. I fought with everything in me! I fought to open the door, but as soon as I did, he reached over me and slammed it shut. He overpowered me and I had no more strength to fight. I felt my mind go to another place because I could not deal with what was happening. Afterwards, I felt so helpless and hurt. He dropped me off at home and now I was even more broken. I could not tell anyone. I was so ashamed and heartbroken. Although I did not know what sex was at the time, I knew it was not right and it made me feel dirty. I took a long shower. I cried quietly as I tried to wash the dirty feeling away. As I laid in my bed and cried into my pillow, I thought that if this boy knew that my daddy was in the house, he would've never dared to touch me that way. I could have screamed, "I'm gonna tell my daddy!" Where was my daddy? I did not know. Why was he not there to protect me and keep this from happening to me? He just did not care. I did not matter to him and I was not worthy or valuable to him. TRASH! I felt like TRASH. TRASH that he did not care about. If my daddy did not love me before, how will he love me now that I am dirty and broken? Now I found it hard to hold my head up at all. My shell totally closed and no one was allowed in. I no longer had a best friend. I was all alone. I knew everyone that I went to school with, but I did not hang out with anyone. I went to school, did my work, and went home. I was broken and I did not know how to fix myself. I did not feel that God even loved me. How could he, my daddy did not love me, why would God care about me. The fact remained though, deep in my heart, I still loved them both.

The first time that God showed me that I had to forgive in order to move on was when I was around thirteen or fourteen. The phone rang and my mother answered it. Immediately I knew that something was very wrong from the tone of her voice. She hung up the phone and called us all together. She told us that my father had a horrible accident and was in the hospital. She told us that he had severed some of his fingers in the lawn mower as he tried to pull a string that had gotten entangled in the mower and it quickly pulled his hand into the mower. I felt really sorry for my daddy, but I was still angry. I prayed intently for him, but I did not want to go and see him. My mother kept asking me when I was going to see my father, but I kept telling her I was not ready. The third day she called me into her room and sat me down. She told me that no matter what my daddy had done, he was still my father and I would have to eventually forgive him for hurting me. She said that even though I had been abandoned, alone and fatherless, I was never without Our Father. She explained that He was there keeping me through it all. But now I had some work to do. She opened her bible and read Colossians 3:13, "Bear with each other and forgive one another if any of you has a grievance against someone. Forgive as the Lord forgave you." She told me that God is not pleased when we hold things against others, because we all make mistakes. She told me that God had an expectation for us to forgive and treat others the way that we want to be treated. She told me that God sees all of our sin and He will decide the punishment for our sin, not us. I blurted out "But he hurt you too, and now you have to work so hard." My mother smiled and said "I forgave your father a long time ago, because when you do not forgive it is like carrying around a bag of heavy rocks everywhere you go. That is very heavy after a while. When you forgive them, it is like dropping that bag and feeling the freedom and the peace of God." She said I could continue to be angry and unforgiving but God was watching and the next time I mess up, God would not forgive me. Also, she reminded me that I would continue to carry that heavy bag of rocks and God would be shaking His head at me in disapproval.

I felt really bad about holding on to hurt and not forgiving, when I knew that I had messed up plenty of times. I really wanted that peace that my mom was talking about. I needed it. I remembered sitting in the room and asking God to help me forgive my daddy that I loved dearly deep down in my heart, somewhere. I clearly heard God say that "I will fix you and give you peace when you forgive him." I remembered thinking that I did not know that I was broken, but now I knew that I was and I had been broken since my father left. I needed to do what God asked of me and He would fix everything. I was actually excited to go to the hospital the next day. I asked to stop at the store and I anxiously searched for a beautiful and loving card for my daddy. I found the perfect card and presented it to my father that day and it brought tears to his eyes. At that moment I felt that peace that my mom spoke of and I could see my daddy that I loved with all my heart laying in that bed. I had forgiven him and we would talk occasionally. I knew that I was free of my anger of being left fatherless and it felt amazing.

God sent me my soul mate at the end of my tenth grade year. I would have probably spent the rest of my life in a shell if God had not sent this persistent, determined, strong-minded boy to rescue me. I met him one day after school as I waited for my brother to pick me up. He was so confident in himself that he scared me. He told me on the first day that he met me that I was going to be his wife. Fear made me freeze. I was so afraid that I jumped in the car with my friend so that I would not be left there with him. He was a student at another school, but he would come to my school at lunch time and look for me. I would literally hide from him. The more I pushed him away, the more he pursued me. Every time I told him no, he would come back again and again. I feared that he would find out my secret that I had been raped. I thought that he would see that I was dirty and not worthy of being loved. I did not want to be rejected again, not ever. I felt that he would leave me like my father did. Yet he still pursued.

Finally, after months of him hunting me down, I decided to give him a chance. This was only because I found out that he was caring for his grandmother, and that he was so sweet, kind and tender towards her. At first, I did not trust him and I would not talk to him, but he did not care, he would talk to me anyways. With time, I became fond of him and I began to fall for him. Now, I had a protector and someone to love me even though my daddy was not there to do it.

Even though I found the love of my life, growing up as a fatherless daughter had taken a toll on me and it affected my marriage, my relationship with my children, and the way I interacted with men. In addition, I had trust issues, and I literally feared male authority figures. Even though I had truly forgiven my father, I still had many strongholds in my life because of my fatherless years. In my marriage, it was hard for my husband to get really close to me, and at times I would push him away. This was because my self-esteem was low and I figured that he would eventually leave at some point. Being fatherless made me feel worthless all my life and I never wanted my sons to feel that. We had five sons and I endured a lot to hold my marriage together so that they would not have to worry about felling worthless and unwanted. When my marriage got unbearable and painful to me, I would bear it so that my sons would always have their father. I felt that if I left him he would not come back to see them as my father had done to me. They would not be broken in the way that I was broken. Also, I was overly protective of my sons in my mind, was making sure that they felt loved and protected. Having been abandoned by my father and raped because no one was there to protect me, I was going to do everything that I could to cover my children from this hurt and pain.

While at church one Sunday, our pastor was preaching on strongholds and how we have to clean them up so that we can be prepared to walk in the purpose that God had prepared for us. He said that many strongholds are residual issues from being deeply hurt. We have to find a way to deal with the hurt and pain, and it causes us to find ways to cope. This was exactly what I needed at that time of my life. I knew that I needed to fix the issues of my past. I sat down and wrote out everything that I thought and did that was caused by my fatherless years. I had to ask God to help me repair this damage in all the areas of my life that were not pleasing to Him. Thus began my first purging. God began to show me everything that I needed Him to fix in me. He began to restore my self-esteem, my fear of men, my issues with overprotecting my sons, trust issues, male authority issues and the list goes on. God set me free of these strongholds that I struggled with over the years and I thank Him for that.

When I was in my mid-thirties, my daddy began to come to my house regularly and spend time with us. We repaired our broken relationship and we were able to spend more quality time together. I still wanted and needed this relationship with him. My sons simply adored him as I had as a child. He would come and they would laugh and talk to him for hours. He was an awesome grandfather to my children and he remained in their lives until he passed away in 1997. He dropped the ball with me, but he got it right with his grandchildren and that was all right with me.

One thing I learned and has stuck with me is that forgiveness is necessary for every hurt. All hurt carries a certain level of anger.

The longer we hold on to hurt and not forgive, the more that anger grows. This anger will not only be directed toward the person who hurt you, but also spills out onto other innocent people. I thank God for using my mother to teach me that forgiving is the right thing to do in God's eyes. She told me of the peace that it would bring and this was so true because I experienced that peace immediately upon forgiving my daddy for leaving me. Even if I had never gotten the opportunity to speak to my father again after I forgave him that day, the peace of God moved in my heart and I was set free. Also, the sermon by my pastor, whom I love dearly, taught me to clean up my stronghold or residual mess. What we do not acknowledge, we will never be able to expel. Taking the time to write out all of my issues that this deep fatherless hurt had deposited in my life changed and blessed me in so many ways. Looking back and facing all of the hurt, pain and the big hole that it left in my life for so many years, I would gladly endure it all to be able to share my story and help one person to overcome their pain. Now I would never have thought that my pain and misery would turn into a blessing for someone else. As Romans 8:28 says, "And we know that in all things God works for the good of those who love him, who have been called according to his purpose."

The Impact of Jean's Story on Your Life

What moment in this story resonated with you the most?

____

____

____

____

____

____

How has this story impacted you?

____

____

____

____

____

____

Jean Harrison

Jean Harrison is a wife and mother of five sons. She is a former high school teacher and is currently home schooling her 16 year old son and her three year old grandson. Jean is a member of the prison ministry, the evangelism team, and is a part of the Rape, Abuse, and Molestation Survivors (RAMS) ministry at her church. She firmly believes in helping others overcome issues that God has helped her to overcome.

CHAPTER TEN

WORKBOOK SECTION

Your Journey to Love, Acceptance and Forgiveness

Get Ready.
Your Life is About to
Change...

Your Journey of Love, Acceptance & Forgiveness.
It's a Journey Worth Taking!

fatherlessdaughters.net

Greetings!

We hope that you have enjoyed reading the stories of these women who grew up as fatherless daughters. The one thing they all share is that pain of not having a loving and attentive father.

Yet, something else that we all have in common is the ability to heal and make new choices. This section of our book will offer you an opportunity heal and move your life forward.

These short, yet powerful, exercises are taken from our Fatherless Daughter Breakthrough Program. It is our hope that you gain awareness and new skills to deal with any daddy wounds and find the courage to move forward onto a journey of love, acceptance and forgiveness.

Before You Get Started!

Watch Our Video and Take our online Fatherless Daughter Archetype Assessment Quiz at www.fatherlessdaughters.net

Once you have completed this step, proceed to the next page to Step One and start your Journey.

Step One:

Re-Awaken to the Truth of Who You Are

Your Defining Moment: When you are willing to let go of who you are not, step into your most powerful space and become who you were born to be.

3 Steps to Re-Awakening Who You Are:

1. Recognize that you are already whole and complete.
2. Let go of the limited picture you have of yourself and begin to immerse in yourself in your own divinity by living within the higher principles of Spirit.
3. Cultivate the right conditions in which you can emerge & unfold naturally as your truest self.

Assignment:

Write a brief description of who you are without giving any reference to your work, your children, your mate or family. These are all titles that you hold, they are not who you really are. Ask yourself, "who am I?" Begin to write until you can't write any more. Allow yourself to flow and be very descriptive in your writing. As you do this, your self image will become more and more clear.

____

____

____

Step Two:

Release What No Longer Serves You

Your Defining Moment: Realizing that the source of your pain is not what others did to you, but your inability to release, let go and forgive. Acknowledging that this truth releases you from the shackles of the pain and wounds that were inflicted upon you by your father. Releasing and forgiveness then becomes your ticket to freedom.

Steps to Releasing What No Longer Serves You:

1. Make a decision to forgive and unlock the door to change and transformation in your life.
2. Decide to stop playing the victim and move to a space of being victorious in life.
3. Night-Time Forgiveness Ritual:

Make forgiveness a daily process. It's nearly impossible to be completely free of judgment, blame and guilt. Release that load daily. With regular attention to forgiveness (which is an aspect of love) you will see a new accountable and accepting you emerge. If your grievance with your father is deep, you may want to engage in a longer-term practice.

Here's the first. Every night, before going to sleep, relax and become calm. Then, using the name of who or whatever you feel resentment towards, say silently to yourself, with as much sincerity as you can:

"[Name], I fully and freely forgive you. I completely let you go. I do not wish to hurt you. I wish you no harm. As far as I am concerned, this trouble between us is over forever. You are free, and I am free, and all is well again between us."

Second exercise, again relax fully after you get into bed for the night. When your mind is quiet, picture the face of the person you want to forgive, and imagine yourself giving them everything that you would like for yourself. These may not be easy exercises for you to do, if your anger is well anchored. But muster as much sincerity as you can each night. Your heart will gradually open and you will be freed.

Step Three:

Rewrite Your Own Love Story

Your Defining Moment: That I could at any moment change my life and that I had the power to rewrite my own love story.

Steps to rewriting your love story:

1. Decide what you want.
2. Recognize that only what you are not giving is missing. Give that which you seek.
3. What truth have you been telling yourself about your story that you can change by replacing it with a new Truth?

   ____

   ____

   ____

   ____

4. Revive and rewrite your story now.

Loving Yourself Ritual:

Take off all of your clothes and stand in front of a full length mirror. Look at every single part of your imperfect body and see it as being perfect. Then lean in closer to look into your eyes. Don't be surprised at the uneasy feeling you will experience at first glance. You will have an intense urge to stop and not go on, but push past the fear. Lean into the mirror and look yourself squarely in the eyes, say to yourself, "____ I love you." Repeat this process seven times.

A Message to My Father: An Unsent Release Letter

When your challenge is directly connected with another individual, you can hand-write a letter to release the souls and subconscious minds of both you and the other party. You do not have to dwell on the situation in depth in the letter.

Do not send this letter.

A Sample Release Letter:

Address Date

Dear Soul of ...,

I request the release of (fear, anger, pain, frustration, etc) regarding....

I give my subconscious mind and my soul permission to carry out the release of the above misunderstandings and emotions whether they reside in my conscious mind or my subconscious mind.

Thank you for the experiences. I have gained understanding from them and now I let them go for positive transformation.

I forgive (name) and I release him to his highest good.

I forgive myself and I free myself to realize my highest good, freedom, fulfillment of inner dreams, clarity, love, peace, joy, expression and prosperity.

Thank you. Sincerely with love, Name and signature

Step Four

Take the Vow 2 Love

A Vow is a solemn promise and commitment.

Close your eyes, take a nice deep breath and speak aloud the following vow:

"I hereby take this solemn Vow 2 Love myself and to love all others by demonstrating love in all that I think, say and do.

I know that when I forget, all I simply need to do is remember who I am and start anew.

This is my solemn Vow to embrace Love as a lifestyle. And so it is and so it shall be."

Signature____________________ Date_________

Note: Join our Vow 2 Love Movement at: www.Ivow2love.com

THE FATHERLESS DAUGHTERS NETWORK

The World's Leading Premiere Movement for Fatherless Daughters

The Fatherless Daughters Network is a global community of Certified Fatherless Daughter Advocates who aim to elevate the awareness of the negative impact that fatherlessness has on a female's life.

This rapidly growing community of women provide educational services, resources, online and live events designed to combat and decrease the many negative influences in the lives of females who grew up fatherless.

Through monthly, quarterly and annual meetings, activities, workshops, retreats and conferences, lead by our Certified Fatherless Daughter Advocates, women and girls can learn empowering tools for healing old wounds, while finding support and sisterhood.

Based on the teachings of Angela Carr Patterson's groundbreaking work, "The Journey to Being Process™", women and girls will learn how to reawaken who they are beyond their fatherlessness, reclaim their worth and rewrite a new narrative for their lives. Learn more about The Fatherless Daughters Network: www.fatherlessdaughters.net

Angela Carr Patterson

The Fatherless Daughters Network Founder

Angela Carr Patterson is the CEO and President of Oasis Promotions, LLC, a Personal and Professional Development Company. Angela is a speaker, author, tv/radio host, documentarian, Global Life/Success Strategist, Founder of the Fatherless Daughters Network and The Awakened Beauty Movement.

A much sought after and highly magnetic speaker, Angela has graced numerous national stages and international platforms. Recognized for her trademark message, "Awaken Your Truth," Angela uses humor, mixed with wisdom and insight, to help women awaken to the truth of who they really are, actualize the power of self love, and unleash their greatest potential to shine in the world. Learn more about Angela at www.angelacarrpatterson.com.

Made in the USA
Coppell, TX
23 September 2021